Menu Math

**Super-Fun Reproducible Menus With Skill-Building Worksheets
That Give Kids Practice in Addition, Subtraction,
Money, Fractions, Problem Solving, and More**

by Martin Lee & Marcia Miller

SCHOLASTIC

PROFESSIONAL BOOKS

New York • Toronto • London • Auckland • Sydney • Mexico City
New Delhi • Hong Kong • Buenos Aires

**To the real Zoe,
who loves vegetables!**

Cover design by **Josué Castilleja**
Interior design by **Holly Grundon**
Interior Illustrations by **Teresa Anderko**

ISBN 0-439-22725-9
Copyright © 2001 by Martin Lee and Marcia Miller
All rights reserved.
Printed in the U.S.A.

Contents

Menus and Reproducible Worksheets

More Restaurant Reproducibles

Dear Teacher,

Can you remember how exciting it was when you were a child to go to a restaurant and select whatever you wanted from a broad menu of choices? To order something different from what others were eating, or from what you'd normally eat at home? It's exciting for children to make choices, and to imagine that they can select whatever they'd like. *Menu Math* offers this—and more.

Menu Math provides a variety of menus designed to whet children's appetites for math. Some of the menus are straightforward, while others are whimsical, or downright silly! Each menu affords children the chance to apply mathematical skills and thinking to a lifelike situation.

As children work with the data presented in the menus, they will extend mathematical understanding, communicate mathematically, and develop positive attitudes toward applying math in the "real" world. Children will fill out order forms. They will compare and contrast prices, compute with money amounts, determine change and patterns, look for number relationships, use reasoning and problem-solving skills, and apply number sense. They will consider possibilities and combinations. Using *Menu Math* can help children to extend mathematical thinking into the worlds of nutrition, science, language, social studies, fantasy, and in any other direction their imaginations—and yours!—can take them.

Incorporate *Menu Math* into your math curriculum to support and enhance basic skills. Use it as a fun-Friday kind of activity, to stimulate role-playing opportunities and creative play, and as a springboard for language, research, or cross-curricular projects. However you decide to use it in your classroom, *bon appétit*!

—Marcia Miller and Martin Lee

Using This Book

Use the menus, questions, teaching tips, and reproducibles in any way that suits your teaching style, classroom goals, and students' skill levels and learning styles. Here are some suggestions:

Take time to go over the menus with children. Help to familiarize them with the kinds of information, language, organization, and price structures they will encounter.

Each menu is followed by two sets of sample questions. In general, the second set is more challenging. Use any or all of these questions as they are, or as starting points. Make up similar questions or invite children to do so. Children can use play money to help them solve the problems.

Use the menus as class work, homework, or project work. Invite children to add items to the menus. Encourage them to create their own menus and sets of questions, using the menu template on page 60.

For questions with multiple answers, allow students time to share their findings and solution methods with the class or in groups.

Provide calculators for children to use as "cash registers" to verify totals.

Set up a restaurant area in your classroom, if space permits. Children can make placemats (see page 62) or centerpieces to decorate the area. Provide aprons, napkins, plastic silverware, plates, etc. Duplicate the order form on page 59 so children can record their orders, or pretend to wait on classmates.

Maintain a menu collection (in a box, in a folder, on a bulletin board) you gather from local restaurants and take-out places. Invite children to "order in" from time to time, using play money. Role-play the phone call they would make to place the order.

Take a moment to reinforce appropriate restaurant behavior.

Children of this age may not be able to calculate tax or tips, but you can discuss their purpose. To make children's experience more authentic, you may wish to provide simple tables or charts they can refer to as they figure total costs.

Making the Menus
To make menus for each child, simply make double-sided copies of each menu and have children fold in half. Children can then color and decorate their menus.

Teaching Tips

*Try these teaching ideas and strategies
as you experience each menu!*

pages 11-12

Just Snacks

- Have children brainstorm a list of their favorite snacks.

- Have children design a logo for a street stand, or an apron for the vendor.

- Use measuring cups to determine reasonable sizes for each portion.

- Extend by having children add other items and prices to the menu.

pages 15-16

Zoe's Zoo Foods

- Have children model each price with play coins. Encourage them to show the same price using different combinations of coins.

- Challenge children to tell how much change they would get back from one dollar for each purchase of one zoo food.

- Help children look through newspaper ads or catalogs to find out actual prices for some of the items sold at Zoe's, and compare these prices with the prices listed for Zoe's Zoo Foods.

- Extend by helping children find out what each animal eats in the wild.

Double Dare Diner

● Help children see the humor in the menu at Double Dare Diner. Discuss which items sound like "real" foods and which sound like jokes.

● Ask additional questions, such as *What is the cheapest three-course meal you can get at Double Dare Diner?* or *If you ordered sweets at Double Dare Diner, what would you order? How much would you spend?*

● Present a total cost, such as $7. Challenge children to list all possible orders they could make having that total.

Sloppy Stan's

● Take a class poll to determine which is the most (or least) popular snack and sweet at Sloppy Stan's. Present the results in the form of a table or graph.

● Take an imaginary class order and determine the total cost.

● Suppose everyone in the class contributed 25¢ toward buying snacks. *How much money would you collect? What snacks could you then afford at Sloppy Stan's?*

● Make popcorn together. Measure the uncooked kernels. Then measure the popped corn to compare the volume before and after popping. Figure out how much it would cost for the whole class (including you!) to order popcorn from Sloppy Stan's. Then figure out the actual cost.

Mary & Cal's Mixed-Up Café

● Talk about ways to reorganize the mixed-up menu. Children might suggest arranging items by food categories, price, or alphabetical order.

● Work with children to figure out how much it would cost at Mary & Cal's Café to order one cupcake for each person in the class—including you!

● Clarify some of the menu items that children may not know. For example, miso soup is a Japanese item, made from soy beans. Invite children who have tasted some of the less-familiar items to describe them to classmates.

● Challenge children to think up other M and C slogans to add to the menu, or other food items that maintain the M and C theme.

pages 31-32

Good Morning!

● Discuss with the class why breakfast is an important meal.

● Take a poll of children's favorite breakfast meals, side dishes, and drinks. Show the results in a graph or table.

● Brainstorm all the different ways children can think of to have eggs. Then invite children to vote on their favorite style of eggs. Analyze the results.

● Challenge children to figure out how much it would cost to order French Toast for everyone in the class—including you, of course!

● Extend by having children work together to plan a class pancake breakfast. Help them determine how many pancakes it would take to feed everyone in the class, and what else would go with the pancakes to make a complete breakfast. Work together to estimate the total cost, as well as the cost per child.

pages 35-36

Pizza Palace

● Have children plan, conduct, and report on pizza-preference surveys of classmates, family members, and friends.

● Plan a field trip to a local pizza parlor to find out how pizza is made. Have children prepare lists of questions in advance that they can ask the pizza cooks.

● Order pizza for your class from Pizza Palace. Decide how many pies you need. Choose the toppings you like. Ask: *What will we order? What will it cost?*

● Extend by collecting menus from various pizza places in your area. Have groups of children compare and contrast prices, pizza sizes, toppings, delivery charges, and other options.

Big Portions

● Be sure children know that 1 dozen = 12 items. Brainstorm for things that customarily come in dozens, such as eggs, donuts, or bagels.

● Display various quart containers. Have children pour water from the containers into paper cups so they can get a feel for how many servings a quart provides. Then display a bucket and have children guess how many quarts it holds. Use the containers to confirm the guess by measuring and pouring water.

● Have children model clay "foods" that they can practice dividing into halves, thirds, or fourths with a paper-clip "knife."

Kim & Tony's Noodle Shop

● Help children do research to find out about the origin of noodles.

● Invite children to bring in samples of different shapes of pasta or noodles. Display the various shapes on a table or bulletin board. Encourage children to sort and classify the shapes in as many different ways as they can.

● Plan a class pasta party. You can make spaghetti with butter and cheese, or with a simple tomato sauce. Work with children to plan quantities of pasta, water, sauce, paper plates, napkins, and so on.

● Conduct a survey of the children's favorite kind of pasta or noodles. Display the results in a graph or table.

Finicky Fred's

● Help children grasp the meaning of the word *finicky*. Brainstorm with children for other words that convey the same meaning, such as *fussy*, *picky*, or *choosy*.

● Have small groups work together to list foods that they will eat only in particular ways, such as only raw carrots, only white-meat turkey, or hot dogs only with ketchup. Invite groups to share their lists.

● Invite children to add other items to the menu, along with suitable prices.

pages 51-52

Half & Half Café

● Be sure children understand that the given price for each item covers the half. Have them use models or pictures to prove what happens when you double things.

● Discuss the ways you might divide various foods into half portions.

● Have children use paper or clay "foods" to show how they would divide them into equal halves. For instance, discuss the fairest way to cut a wedge-shaped slice of pizza to form two equal servings.

● Invite children to revise actual menus from local restaurants to show the costs of half-portions. Assume that such portions could be made available.

● Extend by having children model adding like fractions to form whole and mixed numbers. For instance, cut oranges into halves. Use the halves to prove that $\frac{1}{2} + \frac{1}{2} + \frac{1}{2} + \frac{1}{2} = 2$;

or that $\frac{1}{2} + \frac{1}{2} + \frac{1}{2} = 1\frac{1}{2}$.

pages 55-56

Sandy's Sundaes

● Take a class survey of favorite ice cream flavors, sundaes, and toppings. Display the results in a graph or chart.

● Ask children to explain how the toppings are listed (in descending price order).

● Have children rearrange the ice cream flavors by listing them in alphabetical order, or in order of word length.

● Collect actual menus from local ice cream shops. Challenge children to figure out the cost of sundaes similar to the ones offered at Sandy's.

Just Snacks

Small Amounts in a
Small Restaurant—
Small Prices, Too!

1

At JUST SNACKS we say,
"There's no order too small!"

4

Small Snacks

Potato Chips .... 60¢

Pretzels .... 45¢

Popcorn .... 55¢

Peanuts .... 50¢

Bagel Bites .... 65¢

Teeny Sandwiches .... 75¢

Cup of Soup .... 40¢

Small Sweets & Drinks

Cookie .... 40¢

Donut Hole .... 25¢

Ice Cream Bar .... 60¢

Raisins .... 30¢

Sip of Milk .... 10¢

Gulp of Juice .... 15¢

Name: _____

Just Snacks

1. Which snack costs the most? _____

    How much do they cost? _____

2. Which sweet costs the least? _____

    How much does it cost? _____

3. **Henry spends 50¢ on a snack.**

    What does he buy? _____

4. **Gina orders a drink. She spends 15¢.**

    Which drink does she order? _____

5. **Dan orders popcorn and a cookie.**

    How much does he pay? _____

6. **Pat buys a cup of soup and a sip of milk.**

    How much does she spend? _____

Name: _____

Just Snacks

1. What costs more: a cup of soup or potato chips?

_____

How much more? _____

2. James buys bagel bites and a sip of milk.

How much does he spend? _____

3. Mai buys pretzels and a gulp of juice.

How much does she spend? _____

4. Ed orders teeny sandwiches and a drink. He spends 90¢.

Which drink does he order? _____

5. Sarah spends 80¢. She buys a donut hole and a small snack.

Which small snack does she buy? _____

6. Lisa orders two small sweets. She spends 70¢.

Which two sweets does she order? _____

_____

The Right Foods
for Animals You Love to Feed—
and the Right Amounts, Too!

1

Zoe says,
"My Zoo Foods will make
you the favorite visitor
of your favorite animals!"

4

Food for BIG ANIMALS

Fish for Seals .... 65¢

Hay for Zebras .... 45¢

Bananas for Apes .... 35¢

Peanuts for Elephants ....50¢

Leaves for Giraffes ....25¢

Lettuce for Llamas ....20¢

Berries for Bears ....30¢

Food for LITTLE ANIMALS

Eggs for Foxes .... 30¢

Fish for Puffins .... 40¢

Seeds for Chicks .... 10¢

Pellets for Parrots............15¢

Carrots for Bunnies ....20¢

"Quackers" for Ducks......25¢

Ivy for Lambs ....35¢

Menu Math page 16   Scholastic Professional Books

Name: _____

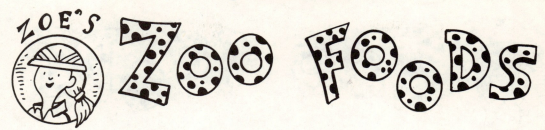

1. How many foods for big
animals does Zoe sell? _____

2. Which foods for little animals cost more than 20¢?

_____

_____

3. **Leon buys hay for zebras and
pellets for parrots.**

How much does it cost in all? _____

4. **Meg buys food for giraffes and for bears.**

How much does she spend in all? _____

5. **Anna buys seeds for chicks.
Alan buys ivy for lambs.**

Who spends more? _____

How much more? _____

6. **Juan buys food for elephants,
llamas, and puffins.**

How much does he spend in all? _____

Name: _____

1. Which two foods for little
animals cost a total of 30¢? _____

_____

2. Which two little-animal foods
together cost less than 40¢? _____

_____

3. **Maude buys food for ducks and for another little animal.
She spends 55¢.**

Which other little animal does she buy food for? _____

4. **Elena buys foods to feed parrots, foxes, and apes.**

How much does it cost her in all? _____

5. **Will buys peanuts and lettuce. Jill buys ivy and hay.**

Who spends more? _____

How much more? _____

6. **Luis spends exactly one dollar on food
for two big animals.**

What are the two animals? _____

Go Ahead – We Dare You!

1

TRY A DARE AT HOME

Order any item from the menu.
Just call us and we will bring it to your door.

Add $2 to the total amount
of your order for delivery.

4

Our Menu

Foods

Surprise Stew $5

Mystery Meatballs $4

Peculiar Pizza $3

Jumping Bean Chili $4

Waxy Waffles $3

Shoe Soup $3

Blue Bread $4

Old Omelette $4

Sweets

Bacon Fudge $3

Inchworm Ice Cream $2

Jellyfish Jell-O $2

Drinks

Sour Soda $1

Muddy Milk $2

Warm Water $1

2   3

Name: _____

1. Which foods and sweets cost $3? _____
_____

2. How many foods cost more than $3? _____
_____

3. What does it cost to buy
Mystery Meatballs and Old Omelette? _____

4. What does it cost to buy all three sweets?
_____

5. What does it cost in all to buy the most
expensive food, sweet, and drink?

_____

6. **Shawn spends $7.**
He buys Blue Bread and a sweet.

Which sweet does he buy? _____

7. Choose a meal you would like.
Pick a food, a sweet, and a drink. _____

_____

What does your meal cost? _____

Name: _____

1. **Sasha buys Waxy Waffles,**
Shoe Soup and Inchworm Ice Cream.

How much does she spend? _____

2. **Greg buys Surprise Stew and Warm Water. Dana**
buys Blue Bread and the most expensive sweet.

Who spends more? _____

How much more? _____

3. **Kia buys Jumping Bean Chili, Bacon Fudge,**
and a drink. She spends $9.

Which drink does she buy? _____

4. **Roy spends $10 on a meal.**
He buys a food, a sweet, and a drink.

What does he buy? _____

5. **Al buys three foods. Each food costs the same.**
He spends $12. He doesn't buy Jumping Bean Chili.
Which three foods does he buy? _____

_____

6. **Suki has $4. She wants to buy one sweet and one drink.**

Which sweet + drink can she buy for $4? _____

What other choice can she make? _____

SLOPPY STAN'S

No Forks! No Spoons!
No Knives! No Kidding!!!
But Lots of FREE Napkins!

1

Sloppy Stan delivers!
He'll even mess up your
kitchen!

4

Snacks

Pretzels & Mustard	$2.25
Buttery Popcorn	$3.25
Slice of Pizza	$2.50
Crispy Taco	$3.00
Cheese Nachos	$3.75
Sloppy Joe	$3.75
Barbecue Ribs	$4.50
Corn on the Cob	$1.00

Sweets

Ice Cream Sandwich	$2.25
Chocolate Fudge	$2.00
Jelly Donut	$1.00
Caramel Apple	$1.25
Filled Cupcake	$1.50
Juicy Peach	$.75
Éclair	$2.75
Cotton Candy	$2.00

Menu Math page 24   Scholastic Professional Books

2

3

Name: _____

Sloppy Stan's

1. How many snacks cost $3 or more? _____

    How many sweets cost less than $2? _____

2. **You buy a sloppy joe and a filled cupcake.**

    How much do you spend? _____

3. **Carl buys the most expensive snack and the cheapest sweet.**

    How much does he spend? _____

4. **You buy a slice of pizza and a jelly donut.
    You pay with a $5 bill.**

    What is your change? _____

5. **Hannah buys a crispy taco and a sweet. She spends $5.75.**

    Which sweet does she buy? _____

6. **Tommy buys two corns on the cob and an ice cream
    sandwich. He pays with a $5 bill.**

    How much change should he get? _____

QUESTIONS-SET 2

SLOPPY STAN'S

1. **David's mom buys 3 slices of pizza. She pays with paper money. Her change is $2.50.**

What bill does she pay with? _____

2. **Teri buys three caramel apples. Inez buys two pretzels.**

Who spends more? _____

How much more? _____

3. **Pick a snack and a sweet that have the same price.**

What do you pay to buy them both? _____

4. **Kevin buys two of the same sweet. He pays with a $10 bill. His change is $5.50.**

What sweet does he buy? _____

5. **Mel and Jane buy a snack to share. Each will have half. Each pays half, too. Each pays $2.25.**

What snack do they share? _____

6. Which snack and sweet would you choose? What would you pay?

_____

_____

Is there another snack + sweet that costs the same? Explain.

_____

Our foods are so good, we can't decide how to list them. But all of our foods start with either M or C.

1

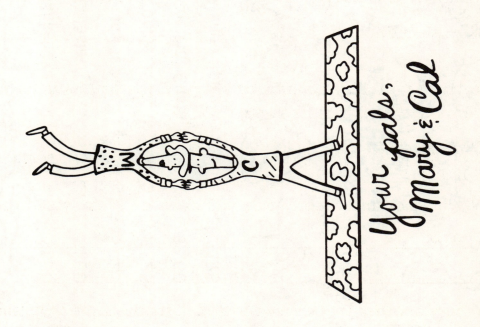

Your pals,
Mary & Cal

4

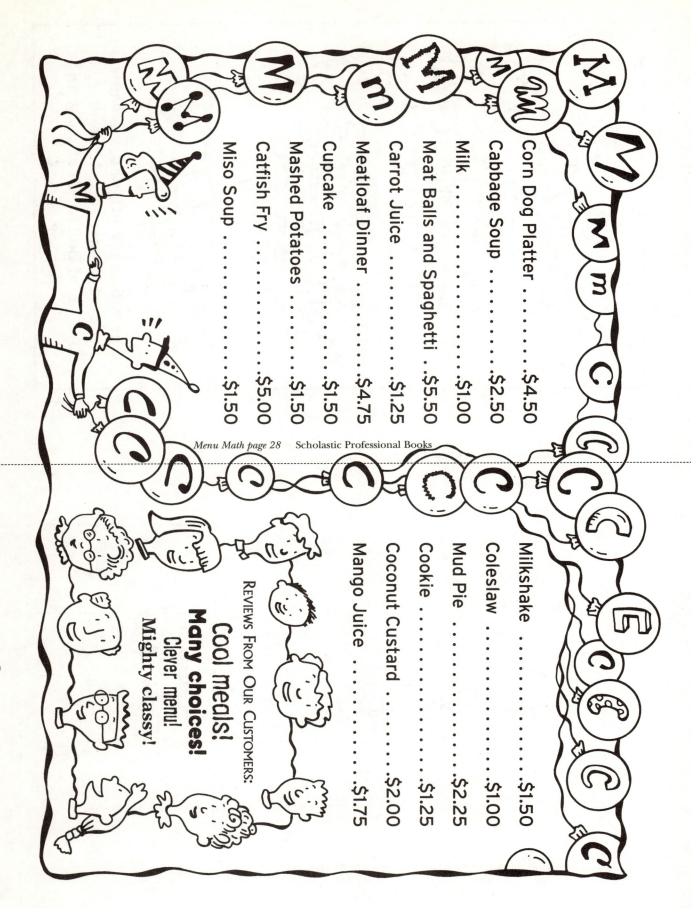

Corn Dog Platter $4.50

Cabbage Soup $2.50

Milk $1.00

Meat Balls and Spaghetti .. $5.50

Carrot Juice $1.25

Meatloaf Dinner $4.75

Cupcake $1.50

Mashed Potatoes $1.50

Catfish Fry $5.00

Miso Soup $1.50

Milkshake $1.50

Coleslaw $1.00

Mud Pie $2.25

Cookie $1.25

Coconut Custard $2.00

Mango Juice $1.75

REVIEWS FROM OUR CUSTOMERS:

Cool meals!
Many choices!
Clever menu!
Mighty classy!

Name: _____

1. How many items start with M? _____

   How many items start with C? _____

2. What fraction of the items
   on the menu start with C? _____

3. How many items on the menu are drinks? _____

   Which drink costs the least? _____

4. What fraction of the items
   on the menu are drinks? _____

5. How many items are desserts? _____

   Which dessert costs the most? _____

6. What fraction of the items are desserts? _____

   What fraction of the items are soups? _____

Name: _____

1. How many items on the menu cost at least $4? _____

What fraction of the items cost at least $4? _____

2. How many items on the menu cost less than $4? _____

What fraction of the items cost less than $4? _____

3. What does a cookie cost? _____

Which soup costs twice that much? _____

4. Which drink costs half as much as coconut custard? _____

What does the drink cost? _____

5. How many items cost more than
$1 but less than $2? _____

What fraction of the items on the menu
cost between $1 and $2? _____

**6. Eat at Mary & Cal's Café. Order four items.
Spend exactly $10.** Which items do you choose?

_____

Egg-stra Good Food to Start Your Day

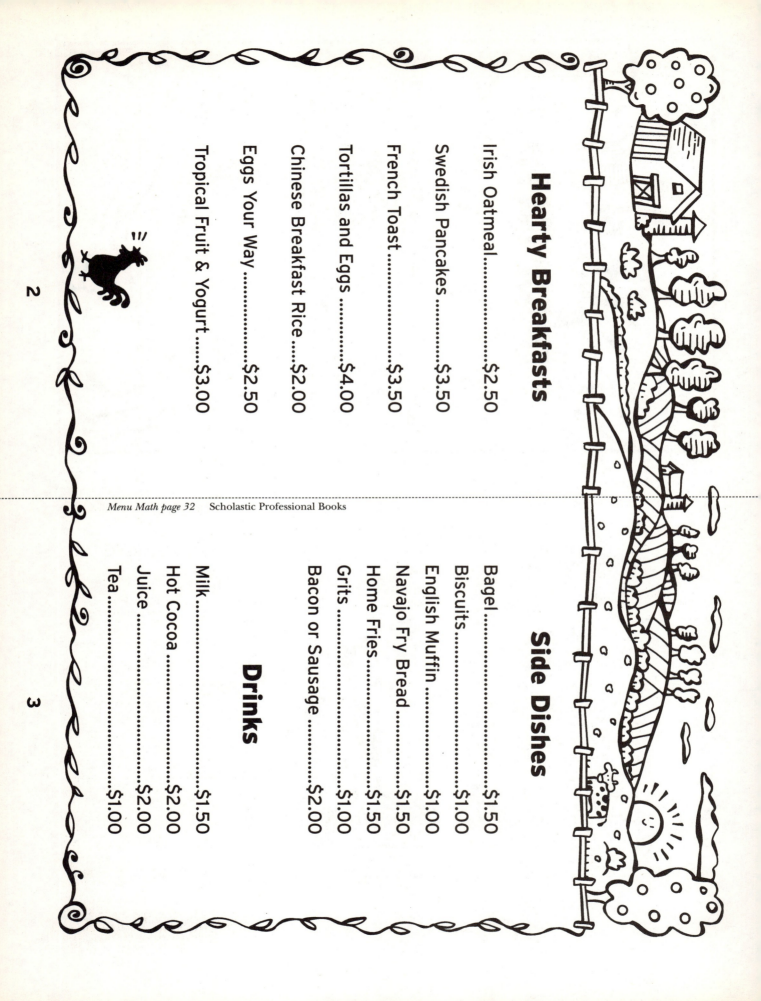

Hearty Breakfasts

Irish Oatmeal $2.50

Swedish Pancakes $3.50

French Toast $3.50

Tortillas and Eggs $4.00

Chinese Breakfast Rice $2.00

Eggs Your Way $2.50

Tropical Fruit & Yogurt $3.00

Side Dishes

Bagel $1.50

Biscuits $1.00

English Muffin $1.00

Navajo Fry Bread $1.50

Home Fries $1.50

Grits $1.00

Bacon or Sausage $2.00

Drinks

Milk $1.50

Hot Cocoa $2.00

Juice $2.00

Tea $1.00

Menu Math page 32 Scholastic Professional Books

Name: _____

1. Which hearty breakfast costs the most? _____

   _____

   Which one costs the least? _____

2. **Mary orders French toast and juice.**

   What does her meal cost? _____

3. **Hiram orders Irish oatmeal, a bagel, and juice.**

   What is the cost of his meal? _____

4. **Jack orders tortillas and eggs and hot cocoa. Danielle orders Chinese breakfast rice, sausage, and milk.**

   Who spends more? _____

   How much more? _____

5. **Paco orders a hearty breakfast with home fries and juice. His meal costs $7.50.**

   Which hearty breakfast does he order? _____

   _____

6. **You have $8 to spend at Good Morning!**
   Order a hearty breakfast, a side dish, and a drink.

   What does your whole meal cost? _____

   What is your change? _____

Name: _____

1. Which hearty breakfast costs the most? _____

Which hearty breakfast costs the least? _____

What is the difference in price? _____

2. **Sam pays $4.50 for tropical fruit & yogurt and a drink.**

Which drink does he order? _____

3. **Warren orders French toast, bacon, and milk. He has a coupon for a half-price meal. He uses it.**

How much does Warren pay for his meal? _____

4. **Jasmine is hungry today. She is also thirsty. She orders Swedish pancakes and Chinese breakfast rice. She orders grits, too. She orders two juices to drink.**

What does her meal cost? _____

5. **Frank takes his two sisters to breakfast. He asks for three orders of Irish oatmeal and three milks. He pays with a $5 bill and a $10 bill.** How much change does he get? _____

6. **You have $6 to spend on a hearty breakfast, a side dish, and a drink.** What do you choose? _____

Do you get any change? Explain. _____

_____

PIZZA PALACE

Where pizza is KING!
We are the tops in toppings!

1

Open daily from
11 a.m. to midnight.

4

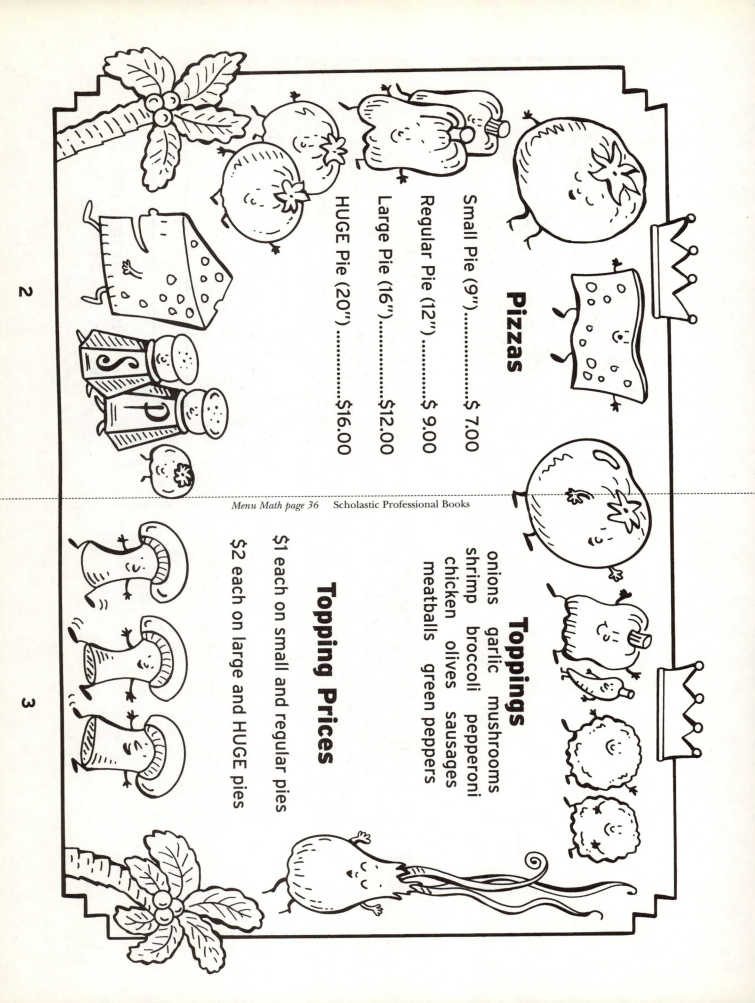

Pizzas

Small Pie (9")...............$ 7.00

Regular Pie (12").........$ 9.00

Large Pie (16")...........$12.00

HUGE Pie (20") $16.00

Toppings

onions   garlic   mushrooms
shrimp   broccoli   pepperoni
chicken   olives   sausages
meatballs   green peppers

Topping Prices

$1 each on small and regular pies

$2 each on large and HUGE pies

2

3

Name: _____

PIZZA PALACE

1. How much is a small pie with two toppings? _____

2. How much is a large pie with one topping? _____

3. **The Klein family buys a regular pie with four toppings. The Chan family buys a regular pie with two toppings.**

   Which family pays more? _____

   How much more? _____

4. Which costs more: a small pie with three toppings or a HUGE pie with no toppings? _____

   How much more? _____

5. **The Molino family orders a large pie with mushroom and pepperoni. They ask for home delivery. They tip the delivery person $2.**

   How much do they pay in all? _____

6. **Choose any size pizza. Pick any number of toppings.**

   What do you choose? _____

   _____

   How much does it cost? _____

Name: _____

PIZZA PALACE

I. Which is cheaper: a small pie with broccoli
or a regular pie with no toppings? _____

_____

How much cheaper? _____

2. **The Kellys order a large pie with mushrooms,
onions, olives, and garlic. What does their
order cost? They pay with a $20 bill.**

Do they get change? Explain. _____

_____

3. **Mike's class orders four large pies. Two pies have
no toppings. Two pies have two toppings each.**

How much does the order cost? _____

4. **The Fuller family is hungrier than usual.
So they order a HUGE pie with everything on it.**

How much does their order cost? _____

5. **The Smiths get a home delivery. They order two large pies
with three toppings on each one. They give a $2 tip to the
delivery person. They pay with two $20 bills.**

How much change do they get? _____

Bring an Appetite!
Bring a Friend! Bring Two!

1

Happy customers say,
"You'll need a wagon to
take home your doggie bag!"

4

Main Courses

Overflowing Bowl of Pasta $10.00

Steak as Big as a Cow $16.00

Yard-Long Hot Dog on BIG Bun ..... $ 9.00

Super-Hero Sandwich $11.00

Jumbo Shrimp (1 dozen!) $14.00

Side Dishes

Tub of Salad $8.00

Bucket of Soup $6.00

Football-Size Potato $3.00

Mountain of Cole Slaw $5.00

2

Drinks

Pitcher of Lemonade $4.00

Quart of Milk $5.00

All the Water You Can Drink .... free!

Desserts

Entire Apple Pie $9.00

Pail of Ice Cream $6.00

Whole Watermelon $5.00

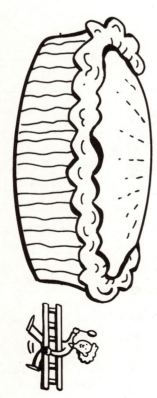

3

BiG PORTIONS

1. **You share the steak with a friend. Each of you pays half.**

How much does each of you pay? _____

2. **Felicia and Clark share a main course and a side dish. The total comes to $14. Each pays half.**

How much does each one pay? _____

3. **Lenny and Jenny share shrimp, soup, and lemonade. Each pays half.**
How much does Lenny pay? _____

4. **Helen and Art share the cost of pasta and a side dish. Each pays $7.50.**
What side dish do they order? _____

5. **You share an entire meal with a hungry friend. You order a main course, a side dish, a drink, and a dessert. You pay half, which is $13.**

What is the total price of the meal? _____

6. **Order a meal to share with a friend. Choose a main course, a side dish, a drink, and a dessert.**

What foods and drink do you pick? _____

_____

How much does each of you pay? _____

BiG PORTIONS

1. **You and two friends share a hot dog. Each of you pays the same amount.**

What is your share of the cost? _____

2. **You and a friend share the cost of steak and ice cream. Each of you gives the server $10. The server frowns at you.**

Why does the server frown? _____

_____

3. **Order a main course, a side dish, and a drink to share with a buddy.**

What do you pick? _____

How much does each of you pay? _____

4. **Choose the cheapest meal that has a main course, a side dish, a drink, and a dessert. Share the cost with a friend.**

What do you each pay? _____

5. **Dana and Fred order a hero sandwich, cole slaw, and milk. Each pays half. Pat, Kit, and Nat order the same meal and share the price equally.**

What will Dana pay? _____

What will Pat pay? _____

Kim and Tony's NOODLE SHOP

Noodles Served Your Way— YOU Decide!

1

Tuesday is New Noodle Night!

Don't Miss It!

4

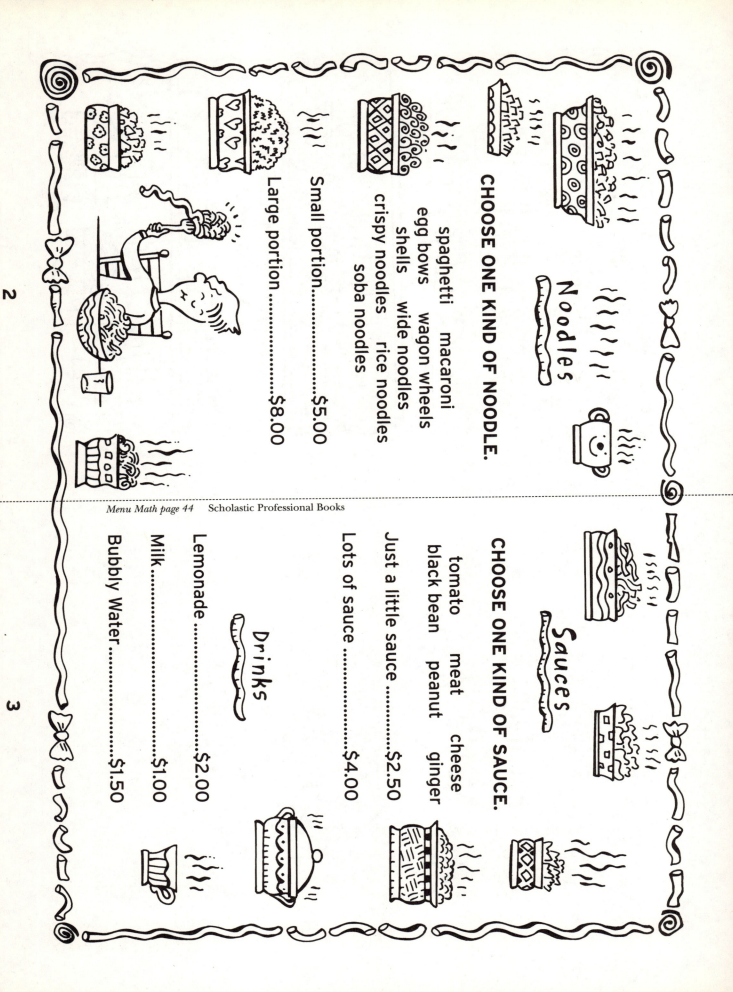

CHOOSE ONE KIND OF NOODLE.

Noodles

spaghetti   macaroni
egg bows   wagon wheels
shells   wide noodles
crispy noodles   rice noodles
soba noodles

Small portion................$5.00

Large portion................$8.00

Menu Math page 44   Scholastic Professional Books

CHOOSE ONE KIND OF SAUCE.

Sauces

tomato   meat   cheese
black bean   peanut   ginger

Just a little sauce $2.50

Lots of sauce $4.00

Drinks

Lemonade $2.00

Milk.........................$1.00

Bubbly Water..........$1.50

Name: _____

Kim and Tony's
NOODLE
SHOP

1. How many different kinds of noodles
can you get here? _____

How many different sauces can you get? _____

2. What is the price for a small portion
of shells with a little tomato sauce? _____

3. What does a large portion of macaroni
served with lots of tomato sauce cost? _____

4. What does a large portion of wagon
wheels with a little meat sauce cost? _____

**5. Deb orders a small portion of
egg bows with lots of cheese sauce.
Miguel orders a large portion of crispy
noodles with just a little ginger sauce.**

How much do Deb and Miguel pay in all? _____

**6. Andre orders a large portion of
soba noodles with just a little sauce.
He also orders lemonade.**
How much does Andre pay in all? _____

Name: _____

Kim and Tony's
NOODLE
SHOP

1. How much is a large order of soba noodles with lots of peanut sauce? _____

2. **Li wants a small portion of shells with just a little cheese sauce. Carmen orders a large portion of rice noodles with lots of black bean sauce.**

   How much do the girls pay in all? _____

3. What costs more: a large portion of noodles with a little sauce or a small portion of noodles with a lot of sauce?

   _____

   How much more? _____

4. **Yoshi orders a small portion of wide noodles with just a little peanut sauce. Maureen chooses a large portion of wide noodles with lots of peanut sauce.**

   Who pays more? _____

   How much more? _____

5. **You order a small portion of egg bows with lots of cheese sauce. You also order bubbly water. You pay with three $5 bills.**

   What is your change? _____

6. **Winona pays $10.50 for noodles in a sauce.** Describe a meal she might get. _____

   _____

Foods for Fussy Eaters

1

4

First

Soup (not too hot) $1.49

Salad (no dressing) $1.99

Chips (no salsa) $1.50

Cheese Sticks (no sauce) $1.39

Main Courses

Pasta (plain) $4.29

Chicken Nuggets (no spices) .. $3.89

Burger (no ketchup or mustard) ...$2.79

Hot Dog (no mustard or relish) ...$2.39

Turkey (no gravy) $4.00

Drinks

Water .... free

Juice (no ice) $1.00

Milk (very cold) $1.29

Iced Tea (no lemon) .... $ .99

Desserts

Plain Vanilla Ice Cream $1.25

Plain Chocolate Pudding ... $1.25

Graham Crackers .... $ .79

Applesauce $1.09

Boring Cookies $1.19

Finicky Fred's

1. What is the most you can pay for a first course? _____

What is the least you can pay? _____

2. What is the price for a hot dog and iced tea? _____

3. **Marco orders chips, a hot dog, water, and ice cream.**

What does he pay for his meal? _____

4. **Will orders soup and a burger.**
Hallie orders salad, turkey, and water.

How much do they pay in all? _____

5. **Tina orders pasta, iced tea, and cookies for dessert.**
Noah orders chips, chicken nuggets, and juice.
He does not order dessert.

Who pays more? _____

How much more? _____

6. **Order one item from each part**
of the menu. Pay with a $20 bill.

What do you order? _____

_____

What is your change? _____

Name: _____

QUESTIONS-SET 2

Finicky Fred's

1. **All Andy wants is salad.**
   So he orders three servings of it.

   Will he pay more or less than $6? _____

   Tell how you know. _____

   _____

2. **You order a first, a main course,**
   a drink, and a dessert.

   What is the most your meal can cost? _____

3. **Krista has a coupon for $2.00 off any main course.**
   She orders cheese sticks, turkey, milk, and pudding.

   What does her meal cost? _____

4. **Eddie orders a first and a main course.**
   His order comes to just a little more than $6.

   What foods has he ordered? _____

5. **Daria orders a burger, iced tea, and graham crackers.**
   She says that the order will come to less than $5.

   How does she know this? Explain. _____

   _____

6. **Order one item from each part of the menu.**

   What do you order? _____

   Oops! You have only $4. How much more money do you need?

   _____

**Half-Size Portions
for the Not-So-Hungry!**

**If you are really hungry,
talk to your server.**

**You can get a full portion—
just double the price!**

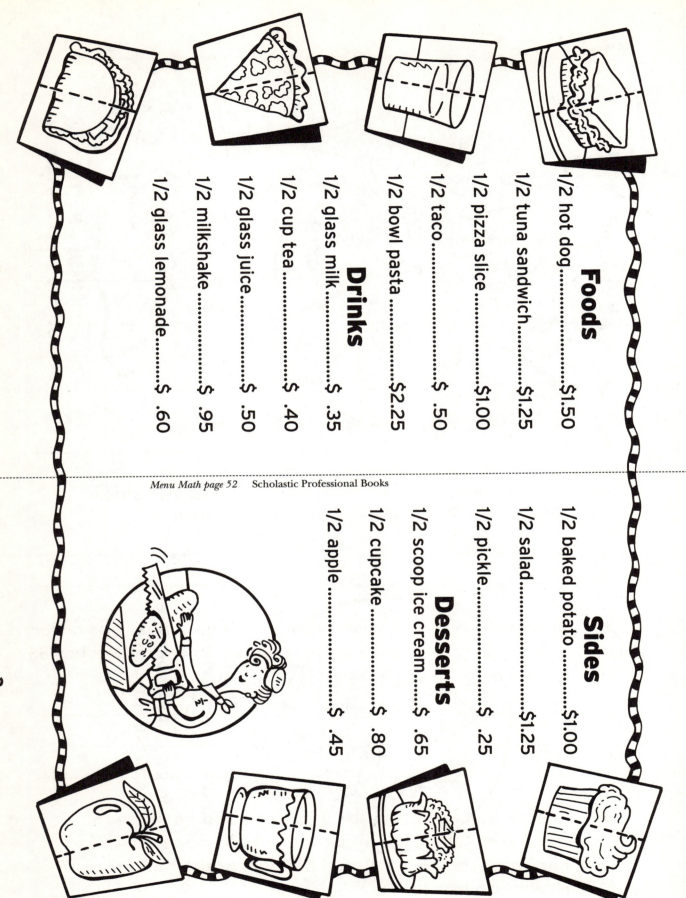

Foods

1/2 hot dog $1.50

1/2 tuna sandwich $1.25

1/2 pizza slice $1.00

1/2 taco .... $ .50

1/2 bowl pasta $2.25

Drinks

1/2 glass milk .... $ .35

1/2 cup tea .... $ .40

1/2 glass juice .... $ .50

1/2 milkshake .... $ .95

1/2 glass lemonade .... $ .60

Sides

1/2 baked potato $1.00

1/2 salad $1.25

1/2 pickle .... $ .25

Desserts

1/2 scoop ice cream .... $ .65

1/2 cupcake .... $ .80

1/2 apple .... $ .45

Name: _____

QUESTIONS-SET 1

Half and Half Café

1. Which item on the menu costs the most? _____
   Which one costs the least? _____

2. How much is half a taco
   and half a glass of lemonade? _____

3. How much do you pay for half a
   pizza slice, half a glass of juice,
   and half a cupcake? _____

4. **Norman orders half a tuna sandwich and two sides.
   He pays $2.75.** Which two sides does he order?

   _____

   _____

5. **Amy is hungrier than she thought. She doubles her order
   of half a hot dog, half a salad, and half an apple. She has $5.**
   Is that enough money? Explain.

   _____

   _____

   _____

6. **Ollie is half as hungry as he thought. So he shares a
   meal with Julie. They share half a bowl of pasta, half a
   lemonade, half a salad, and half a cupcake.**
   How much does each pay? _____

Half and Half
Café

1. **The prices at Half & Half are cheap.**

   How many items on the menu cost less than a dollar? _____

   What fraction of all items cost less than a dollar? _____

2. **Suppose the owners of Half & Half double their prices.**

   What would the most expensive item on the menu cost? _____

   What would the cheapest item cost? _____

3. **Kent orders half a bowl of pasta and half a salad.**
   Nick orders half a taco, half a pickle, half a glass of milk,
   and half a cupcake.

   Whose order costs more? _____

   How much more? _____

4. **Tony has a sweet tooth. He orders each of the desserts.**
   He pays with a $5 bill. What is his change? _____

5. **Liz orders half a hot dog, half a milkshake, half a baked**
   potato, and half a cupcake. She knows that $5 is enough
   money for her order. Explain how she knows this.

   _____

   _____

   _____

6. **Order an item from each part of the menu.**

   How much change do you get if you pay with a $10 bill?

   _____

Make your own sundaes at Sandy's.

SANDY'S SUNDAES

1

Our Treats are hard to beat!

4

Flavors

Vanilla
Chocolate
Strawberry
Coffee
Mint Chip
Peach
Pistachio
Cherry
Fudge Ripple
Berry Swirl
Maple Pecan
Peanut Butter

Ice Cream Prices

One Scoop	$2.00
Two Scoops	$3.50
Three Scoops	$5.00
Four Scoops (Really?)	$6.50

Toppings, Etc.

Hot Fudge	$1.50
Whipped Cream	$1.25
Strawberries	$1.00
Caramel Sauce	$1.00
Marshmallow	$1.00
Bananas	$1.00
Nuts	$ .75
Sprinkles	$ .50

Napkins–free!

Menu Math page 56   Scholastic Professional Books

Name: _____

SANDY's SUNDAES

1. How many different flavors does Sandy sell? _____

How many different toppings? _____

2. What does a sundae that has
one scoop of ice cream
with bananas on top cost? _____

3. What is the price of a sundae that
has two scoops of ice cream,
hot fudge, and sprinkles? _____

**4. Sid orders a sundae that has a scoop of vanilla ice cream
and a scoop of peach ice cream. It has caramel sauce and
whipped cream.**

How much does Sid pay for his sundae? _____

**5. Ivan gets a three-scoop sundae with marshmallow and
sprinkles. Vera gets a sundae with two scoops of ice
cream, strawberries, hot fudge, and nuts.**

Whose sundae costs less? _____

How much less? _____

6. Describe a sundae you would order.

_____

How much does it cost? _____

Name: _____

SANDY's SUNDAES

1. **Rita orders a sundae with one scoop of vanilla ice cream and one topping. Her sundae costs $3.25.**

   What topping does she choose? _____

2. **Angelo orders a sundae that costs $4.**
   It has only sprinkles on top.
   How many scoops of ice cream does it have? _____

3. **Ben's sundae has two scoops of ice cream and two toppings. It costs $6.25.** What are the two toppings?

   _____

4. **Meg will spend exactly $3 on a sundae with cherry ice cream.**
   List the sundaes she might choose.

   _____

   _____

5. **Tonya wants a sundae with two scoops of peach ice cream and one topping. She doesn't want a topping with fruit.**
   List the sundaes she might make with $14.50.

   _____

   _____

6. **Omar will pay $6 for a sundae with vanilla ice cream and one topping.** List the all the sundaes he can make.

   _____

   _____

ORDER FORM

Restaurant _____

Waiter _____ **Number of Customers** _____

QUANTITY	ITEM	PRICE
	TOTAL	

Starters

_____ ·········· $ _____

_____ ·········· $ _____

_____ ·········· $ _____

_____ ·········· $ _____

Main Dishes

_____ ·········· $ _____

_____ ·········· $ _____

_____ ·········· $ _____

_____ ·········· $ _____

Side Dishes

_____ ·········· $ _____

_____ ·········· $ _____

_____ ·········· $ _____

2

Drinks

_____ ·········· $ _____

_____ ·········· $ _____

_____ ·········· $ _____

_____ ·········· $ _____

Desserts

_____ ·········· $ _____

_____ ·········· $ _____

_____ ·········· $ _____

_____ ·········· $ _____

_____ ·········· $ _____

3

Name of Restaurant

1

4

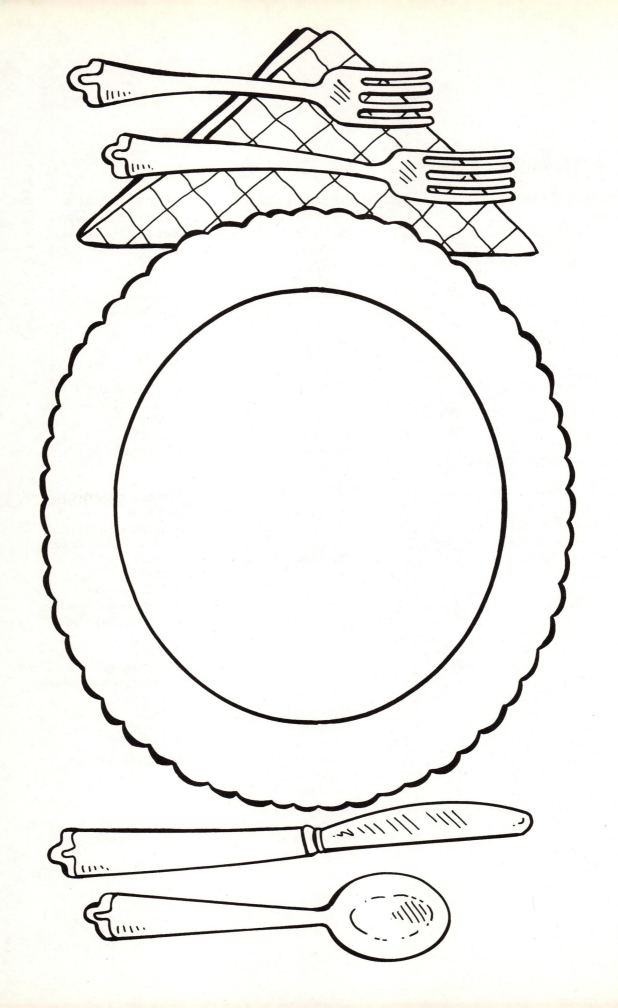

Answers

Just Snacks

Set 1
1. Teeny Sandwiches; 75¢
2. Donut Hole; 25¢
3. Peanuts
4. Gulp of Juice
5. 95¢ 6. 50¢

Set 2
1. Potato Chips; 20¢ more
2. 75¢
3. 60¢
4. Gulp of Juice
5. Popcorn
6. Cookie and Raisins

Zoe's Zoo Foods

Set 1
1. 7
2. Eggs for Foxes,
   Fish for Puffins,
   Quackers for Ducks,
   Ivy for Lambs
3. 60¢
4. 55¢
5. Alan; 25¢
6. $1.10

Set 2
1. Seeds for Chicks + Carrots
   for Bunnies
2. Seeds for Chicks +
   Pellets for Parrots;
   Seeds for Chicks +
   Carrots for Bunnies;
   Seeds for Chicks +
   Quackers for Ducks;
   Pellets for Parrots +
   Carrots for Bunnies
3. Foxes
4. 80¢
5. Jill; 10¢
6. Seals and Apes

Double Dare Diner

Set 1
1. Peculiar Pizza,
   Waxy Waffles, Shoe Soup,
   Bacon Fudge
2. 5
3. $8
4. $7
5. $10
6. Bacon Fudge
7. Answers will vary.

Set 2
1. $8
2. Dana; $1
3. Muddy Milk
4. Surprise Stew, Bacon Fudge,
   Muddy Milk
5. Mystery Meatballs, Blue
   Bread, Old Omelette
6. Answers will vary.

Sloppy Stan's

Set 1
1. 5; 4
2. $5.25
3. $5.25
4. $1.50
5. Eclair
6. 75¢

Set 2
1. $10 bill
2. Inez; 75¢ more
3. Corn on the Cob +
   Jelly Donut or Pretzels +
   Ice Cream Sandwich;
   $2.00 or $4.50
4. Ice Cream Sandwiches
5. Barbecue Ribs
6. Answers will vary.

Mary & Cal's Mixed-Up Café

Set 1
1. 8; 8
2. 8/16 or 1/2
3. 4; milk
4. 4/16 or 1/4
5. 4; Mud Pie
6. 4/16 or 1/4

Set 2
1. 4; 4/16 or 1/4
2. 12; 12/16 or 3/4
3. $1.25; Cabbage Soup
4. Milk; $1.00
5. 7; 7/16
6. Answers will vary.

Good Morning!

Set 1
1. Tortillas and Eggs;
   Chinese Breakfast Rice
2. $5.50
3. $6.00
4. Jack; 50¢ more
5. Tortillas and Eggs
6. Answers will vary.

Set 2
1. Tortillas and Eggs; Chinese
   Breakfast Rice; $2.00
2. Milk
3. $3.50
4. $10.50
5. $3
6. Answers will vary.

Pizza Palace
Set 1
1. $9
2. $14
3. Klein; $2
4. Huge pie with no toppings; $6
5. $18
6. Answers will vary.

Set 2
1. Small pie with broccoli; $1
2. $20; they get no change
3. $56
4. $38
5. $2

Big Portions
Set 1
1. $8
2. $7
3. $12
4. Cole Slaw
5. $26
6. Answers will vary.

Set 2
1. $4.50
2. The total is $22, so you are $2 short.
3. Answers will vary.
4. $8.50
5. $10.50; $7

Kim & Tony's Noodle Shop
Set 1
1. 9; 6
2. $7.50
3. $12.00
4. $10.50
5. $19.50
6. $12.50

Set 2
1. $12.00
2. $19.50
3. large portion with a little sauce; $1.50
4. Maureen; $4.50 more
5. $4.50
6. Accept any answers with a large portion of noodles and just a little sauce.

Finicky Fred's
Set 1
1. $1.99; $1.39
2. $3.38
3. $5.14
4. $10.27
5. Tina; 8¢ more
6. Answers will vary.

Set 2
1. less, because one order of salad is less than $2.
2. $8.82
3. $5.93
4. pasta and salad
5. If you round each price to the nearest dollar, you get $3 + $1 + $1 = $5; since all the prices are less than the rounded amount, the total will be less than $5.
6. Answers will vary.

Half & Half Café
Set 1
1. 1/2 bowl pasta; 1/2 pickle
2. $1.10
3. $2.30
4. 1/2 salad and 1/2 pickle
5. No; the total is $6.40, so she is $1.40 short
6. $2.45

Set 2
1. 10; 10/16, or 5/8
2. $4.50; 50¢
3. Kent's order costs more; $1.60
4. $3.10
5. If you round each price up to the nearest dollar, the total would be $5; but each item (except for the hot dog) costs less than the rounded amount, so $5 will be enough.
6. Answers will vary.

Sandy's Sundaes
Set 1
1. 12; 8
2. $3.00
3. $5.50
4. $5.75
5. Ivan's; 25¢
6. Answers will vary.

Set 2
1. Whipped Cream
2. 2
3. Hot Fudge and Whipped Cream
4. Ice cream + strawberries or caramel or marshmallow or banana or two servings of sprinkles
5. Answers will vary.
6. Sample answers: 3 scoops of vanilla + strawberries or caramel or marshmallow or banana; or 2 scoops of vanilla + hot fudge + marshmallow